DEDICATED TO MY FAMILY

This book is dedicated to my parents, my sister and my brother-in-law. Thank you for believing in me, supporting me and hiking with me. I would be lost without you all.

SPECIAL THANKS:
JEFF KNESEBECK FOR THE ENCHANTED VALLEY PICTURE

ABOUT THIS GUIDEBOOK

The Olympic Peninsula.

We created this guidebook for one reason: to give you a hike you can do every week of the year.

The Olympic Peninsula features temperate rainforests, glacial rivers full of salmon and thousands of miles of trails. It is hard to figure out why people live anywhere else in the world. Yes, some areas of the Olympic Peninsula do get well over 10 feet of rain a year, but other areas get less than 20 inches. The Olympic Peninsula is one of the most diverse locations in the world for hikers and climbers and we want you to explore every inch of this beautiful area.

The Olympic Peninsula boasts hundreds of great trails. We picked 52 trails – 363 miles of hiking – that give you the best possible experience. From treeless ridgelines to insanely green rainforest trails, and everything in between, we are sure you will find a few favorites. To make the areas more appealing, we have provided numerous pictures for your enjoyment.

Deciding which hike to try can be difficult, so we broke down the list into three categories: Easy Hikes, Moderate Hikes and Advanced Hikes.

Easy Hikes are easy based on elevation gain and accessibility. Some are longer than five miles, some are shorter, but all are mostly flat. With over 74.5 miles of Easy Hikes, we are sure you will find a few favorites.

Moderate Hikes comprise over 118.4 miles of trails. You are sure to go to some amazing locations. These hikes tend to have more elevation gain and are more remote, but most are manageable for new hikers.

Advanced Hikes are the hardest trails. In this section we have given you 170.1 miles of amazing climbs and areas to explore. These trails are longer and have some serious elevation gain. These are not recommended for new hikers.

Please Remember:

- Bring your 10 Essentials on every hike

- Check the weather

- Tell someone your itenerary

- Be smart and follow all posted signs

Thank you for buying this book. Have a great hike and enjoy the gorgeous Olympic Peninsula, for this truly is one of the most beautiful places in the world.

EASY HIKES

The following hikes are not only easy on the legs, but are easy on the eyes. With short mileage, little to no elevation gain and amazing destinations, this section is rewarding for beginning hikers looking to explore, moderate hikers looking for an easy day and even for advanced hikers looking for a quick afternoon romp through the woods.

Hikes are determined to be easy based on level of ease. Not all easy hikes hikes are family friendly, so please know your limits.

We hope you enjoy these easy hikes, which can be done year round with little to no snow in the winter.

SPIDER LAKE

Spider Lake

Nearest City: Shelton
Best Season: Fall
How Far: 2 Miles
Elevation Gain: 200ft

Directions:
Take Highway 101 to the Skokomish Valley Road .Turn west on the Valley road and drive about 5.5 miles to the junction with FS Road #23. Turn right and proceed for 10 miles on FS Road #23 to the junction of FS Road #2353. Veer left and continue on FS Road #23 another 8 miles to the Spider Lake Trailhead and Spider Lake.

Tucked away in the wilderness known more for Sasquatch sightings and logging, Spider Lake is conveniently located at the midway point between the Olympic Peninsula's two largest dammed lakes. Sitting between Lake Cushman and Wynoochee Lake, Spider Lake is home to stories of mythological beasts; and seeing this trail in the mist or fog, it is easy to see why such stories exist.

With old growth forests along the banks of an easy to get to high alpine lake, this trail should be more popular. At only 2 miles long and an elevation gain of 250ft, this trail is the perfect day hike because it serves as a microcosm of the Olympic Peninsula. While other trails put miles on your legs, Spider Lake gives you the chance to see giant ferns, along with cedar and fir trees towering over bluish green water, stocked full of salamanders. This is seriously one of the more gorgeous trails in this area, and you need to add it to your list.

The trail is maintained for the most part, but be aware that during spring and fall months, downed trees may hinder your hike. In the summer, the bugs can be bad, but typically are less than any other lake. In the winter, this lake will occasionally start to freeze. Seeing the huge trees with snow on them, with a thin layer of ice around the banks of the lake will be a lasting memory.

MURHUT FALLS

Murhut Falls

Nearest City: Hoodsport
Best Season: Spring
How Far: 1.5 Miles
Elevation Gain: 300ft

Directions:
On 101 along the Hood Canal, turn west at milepost 310 onto Duckabush Road. Drive 6.3 miles. You will pass the Collins Creek Campground and go over the Duckabush River Bridge. Bear right at the road junction, signed Murhut Falls Trail. The 1.3 miles remaining on gravel road takes you to the trailhead.

Murhut Falls is gorgeous, falling 130 feet in a two-tier falls. If one is daring, the falls can be climbed down to and played upon. This dog-friendly, kid-friendly, family-friendly trail is just a few miles long, and takes you into the Olympic Peninsula wilderness with little effort. This can be hiked year round, as it is roaring in the Spring, cooling in the winter, gorgeous in the fall and occasionally frozen in the winter months.

The trail to Murhut Falls is not flat, but it is fairly easy. You climb up at the beginning at a somewhat steep angle; but once you do this, you level off then drop back down to the falls. At a mile long, this trail is great for all ages, and dogs are welcome. (There are no restrooms however, so plan ahead!)

In the summer months, this is a great place to climb around, explore and have a picnic. In the winter, ice is everywhere, and the scramble off the trail, which leads to good photo areas, is slippery, dangerous and difficult for beginners to climb. If you want to explore the main falls, climb over the log at the end of the trail and carefully work your way around. Logs and rocks can be used as bridges. For a safer exploration of the lower stream, watch for a slightly steep animal trail a few hundred feet from the falls. This is a remote area perfect for wading, napping and having lunch, close to one of the more gorgeous waterfalls on the Olympic Peninsula.

KALALOCH BEACH AND CAVES

Kalaloch Beach and Caves

Nearest City: Kalaloch
Best Season: All
How Far: 2 Miles
Elevation Gain: 0Ft

Directions:
Head North from
Aberdeen along Highway
101 until you reach the
Kalaloch Lodge. Follow
signs to the trailhead.

Kalaloch Beach is one of the iconic beach areas on the Olympic Peninsula, but not because of the hiking. Typically people know it for the campground and the lodge, which sit high on a bluff looking down to the sandy beaches below. If people knew that an awesome hike existed here, this place might be even more crowded on a sunny summer day.

At the beach, head north from the campground, keeping the bluffs and Highway 101 to your right. The road is near, but after about a mile, the noise fades away as the beach gets protected by bluffs and trees. This hike needs to be done as the tide is going out, so check the tides before you start hiking. At high tide, the views are nice, but access to caves and tide-pools is not available. At low tide, the caves, some with a roof of tree root, are fun to explore, as are the tide-pools, which are full of colorful starfish and sea anemones.

If hikes on the beach aren't your cup of tea, try this hike during the winter, when wind and heavy rains dump down from the sky, and sea foam and giant waves crash along the beach. This is a local's way to see the Pacific Northwest, and no trip to the area, whether you live nearby or across the world, is complete without walking in the rain, finally understanding just how wet the rainforest really can be.

WEDDING ROCKS

Wedding Rocks

Nearest City: Port Angeles
Best Season: All
How Far: 10 Miles
Elevation Gain: 300ft

Directions:
Turn west on SR 112, continuing for 46 miles to the community of Sekiu. Drive 2.5 miles beyond Sekiu and turn left onto the Hoko-Ozette Road. Follow this paved road for 21 miles to the Ozette Ranger Station and trailhead.

Buried in the coast of the Olympic Peninsula, far from any large city, Starbucks or McDonalds, Lake Ozette and the beaches of Ozette sit, untouched by time. With petroglyphs estimated to be over a thousand years old, and sea-stacks that are slowly fading away with each change of the tide, Wedding Rocks might just be the best stretch of beach you have never heard about.

The trail to Wedding Rocks is straightforward. The hike is through the woods for 3 miles and then hiking along the beach for another mile and a half. The trail through the woods can be slick, muddy and difficult in spaces, but typically can be handled by novice hikers. The only real concern you should have along this hike is the tide, as Wedding Rocks is only accessible at low tide. This means you need to plan your trip accordingly, making sure you aren't trapped for a night on the coast.

Wedding Rocks is home to petroglyphs that pre-date the European invasion of America. Take as many pictures as you want, but do not touch them. The oils in your hands will ruin them forever. The fact that they have lasted so long on the brutal Washington Coast is impressive enough, so let us keep them around for future generations. Wedding Rocks is the perfect destination to get away from everything, experience the old culture of the area and view sea life as far removed from society as you can get, at least in the contiguous United States.

CAPE FLATTERY

Cape Flattery

Nearest City: Port Angeles
Best Season: All
How Far: 1.5 Miles
Elevation Gain: 200ft

Directions:
Turn west on SR 112, continuing to the community of Neah Bay. Continue west on Bayview Avenue, following signs for Cape Flattery and Beaches. Turn left on Fort Street, turn right on 3rd Street. Turn left on Cape Flattery Road. In 2.5 miles pass the Tribal Center. Proceed to the trailhead.

Beautifully-designed and maintained by the Proud Makah Nation, the trail to Cape Flattery leads you to one of the most iconic images of the Olympic Peninsula Coast. This trail, which weaves through wonderful old-growth on raised cedar platforms, takes you to the Northwestern-most point in the contiguous United States. With sea stacks and a view of Tatoosh Island, which once was the whaling camp for the mighty Makah tribe, this is an amazing hike no matter what the weather.

Common sights at the end of the Cape Flattery trail are whales, seals, otters, eagles, puffin, and cormorants; but what makes this hike amazing is the view of the coast from the observation deck. The wooden observation deck, raised above the rock and railed for safety gives you a glimpse into the turbulent waters of the Pacific Ocean. The blues of the water, contrasted with the greens of the trees and ferns and browns of kelp makes this more beautiful than any picture can capture.

This is a family-friendly, easy hike that should be done during each season. In the summer and early fall, watch shorebirds and the occasional whale swim by. In the winter, come here for the wind, rain and sheer power of standing in one of the more remote areas in the state. While you are here, stop at Neah Bay, tour the museum and help support the Makah tribe.

FORT FLAGLER

Fort Flagler

Nearest City: Port Townsend
Best Season: All
How Far: 5 Miles
Elevation Gain: Minimal

Directions:
From Port Townsend head west for 5 miles on State Route 20 to SR 19. Continue on SR 19, turning left in 3.5 miles onto SR 116. Follow SR 116 east for 10 miles to its end at Fort Flagler State Park

Normally, we recommend isolated, nature-filled hikes and trails, but Fort Flagler is one of the few exceptions. Fort Flagler, nestled in the northeastern most point on the Olympic Peninsula is a beautiful area that was once used as a training center in WWI. With old mortars, barracks and out-buildings, it is easy to travel back in time and see how war once impacted the Puget Sound.

With water on three sides, this peninsula of a park has over 19,000 ft of saltwater shoreline, as well as views of the Olympic and Cascade Mountains from its bluffs. Most of the buildings are from the early 1900's; and deer, eagles, migratory birds and the occasional whale can be spotted from the park. With interpretive centers open daily from May to October, this is not only a great getaway location, but also a fun, educational destination for families.

At Fort Flagler, you can hike or bike along the five miles of trails in the park and even explore around in the old barracks. If you know or are a military history buff, this is a fantastic place to hike! If military history isn't your thing, this park has something for everyone. You can swim, crab, clam or beach-comb to your heart's content. Spend the day birding, walking through barracks, checking out the museum and then have a fire as the sun sets on what feels like your own private peninsula. With camping available, this is a nice place to go for the weekend or the rare weekday off.

DAMON POINT

Damon Point

Nearest City: Ocean
Shores
Best Season: Winter
How Far: 4 Miles
Elevation Gain: Minimal

Directions: From Ocean
Shores, go south on SR
115 until you reach Point
Brown Avenue in Ocean
Shores. Proceed south on
Point Brown Avenue about
4.5 miles. The entrance is
just past a big abandoned
hotel and RV campground.
Park off the road on the
wide grassy area.

Located on the southernmost point of Ocean Shores, at the base of the Olympic Peninsula, a strip of sand juts out in the Pacific Ocean that serves as a protection barrier for Grays Harbor. On a sunny day from this sand spit, known as Point Brown or Damon Point, one can see the Olympic Mountains, the Pacific Ocean, the inactive Satsop Nuclear Power Plant, and Mt. Rainier. The views aren't the only draw as this is a fantastic place to go birding and beach-combing.

In the winter, after a storm, this beach is one of the best locations for collecting shells, agates, floats and the occasional glass ball. Also in the winter, Damon Point becomes a hot-bed for Snowy Owls and other migratory birds, making it a birders heaven. With eagles, deer and snowy owls to see, this is a perfect hike to do when the rest of the Olympic Peninsula is getting inaccessible with snow. Occasionally, large sea creatures will wash up on the beach, allowing visitors to see whales, jellyfish and more unrecognizable deep sea fish.

While the ideal time to experience Damon Point is during the winter months, the summer months offer awesome views. Occasionally a gray whale will spout in Grays Harbor, and ships, like the Lady Washington (used in numerous Hollywood movies) can be seen sailing around. Kite flying, surfing and wave-jumping are also common and a great way to enjoy one of the most flat, easy walks along the beach. Bring a bag for shells and agates, take the family and enjoy the day on the Washington Coast.

HOLE IN THE WALL

Hole in the Wall

Nearest City: Forks
Best Season: All
How Far: 4 Miles
Elevation Gain: Minimal

Directions:
From Forks, head north
for 2 miles. Turn left on
west on SR 110. In 7.7
miles at Quillayute
Prairie, SR 110 splits.
Take the right fork, Mora
Road, At the road's end
is the trailhead.

If you love the Washington Coast, the hike to Hole in the Wall may just be your ultimate walk along the beach. From miles of giant sea stacks to driftwood and abundant sea life, the walks along the sands of the Olympic Peninsula do not get much better than this. For beach enthusiasts, the sea stacks along this trail, and further along to the Chilean Memorial monument, are far more beautiful than anything along the Oregon Coast.

Along the walk, you will have to cross a few small streams, but typically, there are driftwood bridges created by other hikers. If not, feel free to move a few large longs and branches to create your own bridge. The Hole in the Wall, a sea stack along the shore that is a giant, well, hole in the rock wall, is accessible only during low tide; but the walk along the beach in any tide is well worth the sand in your boots.

In the summer, this beach is amazing! Full of people and tidal life, take your time and explore around in the sun. However, for a true Pacific Northwest experience, check the weather and head out here the day before or after a storm to see rough waves, amazing beach-combing finds and the solitude and beauty that made this land home for the Quileute tribe.

IRELY LAKE

Irely Lake

Nearest City: Aberdeen
Best Season: Spring
How Far: 2 Miles
Elevation Gain: 200ft

Directions:
From Hoquiam travel
north on US 101. Turn
right onto the South
Shore Road. At the
junction with the Quinault
River Bridge, turn left and
cross the bridge. Turn
right onto the North
Shore Road, proceeding
to the parking area
located on your right. The
trail begins on left side of
the road.

While not Lake Quinault, Irely Lake is worth the short walk in the woods. As a family friendly, beginning hike, this is a perfect way to explore the region without getting too far from your comfort zone. This is not a difficult hike, but is one that should be done by everyone.

Irely Lake is underrated and year-round is absolutely gorgeous. With a well-groomed trail leading through dense forests and across rustic old wooden bridges, seeing local flora and fauna is a common experience. During the Spring months, bear activity in the area can be quite high, so make plenty of noise along the way. High ferns and moss-covered trees flank the trail in parts, giving hikers a great experience in the Quinault Rainforest.

A highlight during the Spring months is the nesting birds along the lake. Pileated Woodpeckers constantly fly around the lake, feeding their babies located in holes in trees. Across the lake, an osprey nest looms high in the Douglas Fir trees, with the parents swooping down to catch fish and frogs. Irely Lake is a great place for beginning hikers, children and families, so check it out any time of the year.

MARYMERE FALLS

Marymere Falls

Nearest City: Port
Angeles
Best Season: Spring
How Far: 2 Miles
Elevation Gain: 500ft

Directions:
From Port Angeles
follow US 101 west for
20 miles to Barnes
Point at milepost 228
and turn right. At the
stop sign, turn right and
proceed to a large
parking area. The trail
begins on the
Marymere Falls Nature
Trail near the rustic
Storm King Ranger
Station.

Well-marked, easily-followed and basically a flat walk through the dense forests of the Northern Olympic Peninsula Rain Forest, the Lake Crescent Trail is one of the more popular and scenic trails. Waterfall lovers flock here in the early spring. At 1.5 miles round trip, this trail is less of a hike and more of a walk.

Many people skip out on this hike when the see how crowded it is, but if you decide to go to the falls and battle the crowds, you will be greatly rewarded. After you cross the new metal bridge over the river, the last 400 ft of the trail climbs pretty steadily. Cross a beautiful wooden bridge and start to hike up a ridge that leads you to a great view of Marymere Falls. Take your time walking up this railed path, enjoy the greens of the rain forests and soon you will be given a breathtaking view of a small, yet gorgeous waterfall. At a height of 90 ft, this waterfall is impressive in its simplicity and a perfect short trip after a long day in the car or a relaxing day at the lake.

SPRUCE RAILROAD TRAIL

Spruce Railroad Trail

Nearest City: Port Angeles
Best Season: All
How Far: 8 Miles
Elevation Gain: 250ft

Directions: From Port Angeles follow US 101 West. Turn right onto East Beach Road. Follow this narrow paved road for 3.2 miles. Just beyond the Log Cabin Resort, turn left onto Boundary Creek Road with signs to Spruce Railroad Trail. Follow it for 0.8 mile to the eastern trailhead.

One of the few dog-friendly, family-friendly flat trails in the Olympic National Park, the Spruce Railroad Trail offers one thing that no other trail can, an amazing walk along Lake Crescent. The Second deepest lake in the State of Washington, full of amazing views and history. This trail is ideal for any day of the week.

The Spruce Railroad Trail, which was built as a working railway during World War I, was going to be used to transport Spruce trees to Port Angeles to build airplanes during the war. However, before the railway was completed, the war ended and the forest was not harvested. The trail is long, but flat, making it perfect for the family in nearly any weather. It is almost 8 miles round trip, but it is one of the few trails in any National Park that allows dogs and bikes.

On the Spruce Railroad Trail, one can see many things, ranging from scenic views and railroad tunnels to deep swimming holes and abandoned telegraph poles. One main highlights of the trail, aside from the gorgeous lake and trail tunnels, is the Devil's Punchbowl. During warm weather, the Devil's Punchbowl is the ideal swimming hole. At nearly 100 ft deep, next to the cliff, it is a relatively safe place for swimmers and divers to jump for joy into an alpine lake. The severe drop off at Devil's Punchbowl isn't limited to that area, as Lake Crescent itself is officially 600ft deep. Recent studies have placed the depth over 1000 ft, making this hidden gem even more mysterious.

SOUTH BEACH/QUEETS RIVER

South Beach/ Queets River

Nearest City: Kalaloch
Best Season: All
How Far: 3 Miles
Elevation Gain: 50ft

Directions: 5 Miles South of
Kalaloch Beach and Resort,
along Highway 101

Seeing a river meet the Pacific Ocean is a special event, and on the Olympic Peninsula it is even more awesome. With a short hike along the rugged Washington Coast, feel the sand between your toes as you hike to one of the best salmon rivers in the state. With eagles overhead, walk south to the mouth of one of the more unexplored rivers of the Olympic Peninsula.

During the fall, watch salmon fishermen, eagles, bears and more test their luck and skill trying to get one of the returning salmon. In the summer, this becomes a walk on the beach that is as beautiful as they come. With rocks, shells and other objects washed up on shore, this hike can be done as a family or just a way to experience the coast all by yourself.

DUNGENESS SPIT

Dungeness Spit

Nearest City: Sequim
Best Season: All
How Far: 11 Miles
Elevation Gain: 130ft

Directions: From Sequim head west on US 101 for 5 miles. Turn right at milepost 260 on Kitchen-Dick Road. At 3.3 miles, Kitchen-Dick becomes Lotzgesell Road. In another 0.25 mile, turn left on Voice of America Road and follow the signs to the trailhead.

Jutting out into the Straight of Juan de Fuca, Dungeness Spit is much more than just a long walk on the beach. From watching eagles, herons and migrating birds to seeing migrating whales, cargo ships and kayakers, this may just be the most scenic walk on the beach on the Olympic Peninsula.

The hike is long and flat with the destination being a classic lighthouse standing at the end of the sandbar. This lighthouse is iconic to the region and during sunrise or sunset, you are hard pressed to find a better view. With the Olympic Mountains to the South, Mount Baker to the Northeast and Vancouver Island to the North, the views are spectacular.

Beach-combing, birding and watching for sea life is a must along this hike, but be aware that the area is quite windy. Don't let that stop you though. With shells, agates and an occasional glass ball, this beach is a great place to spend an afternoon or a full day.The hike is extremely kid-friendly, and if you are ever in the area and need something to do, this is an amazing place year round.

PONY BRIDGE

Pony Bridge

Nearest City: Aberdeen
Best Season: All
How Far: 5 Miles
Elevation Gain: 1000ft

Directions:
From Hoquiam travel north on US 101 for 35 miles. Turn right onto the South Shore Road, located 1 mile south of Amanda Park. Proceed on this road for 13.5 miles, coming to a junction at the Quinault River Bridge. Continue right, proceeding 6.2 miles to the road's end and the trailhead.

While the Hoh rainforest gets all the glory, the Quinault Rainforest gets the beauty. To best explore the beauty on a quick day hike, Pony Bridge, located at the Graves Creek Trailhead, is a great destination. While this trail doesn't offer the giant trees that you get a few more miles toward the Enchanted Valley, it does offer a view of a gorge that is so beautiful it will take your breath away.

Pony Bridge is over the Quinault River, and while most bridge crossings in the Olympic National Park are decent, this one ranks among one of the most memorable. Twenty-five feet above a narrow gorge, greenish water is surrounded by moss-covered rock walls and towering trees. Opening up downstream, those more inclined to walk off trail can sit along the fast moving current for a unique lunch.

In the early spring, the river is running high and rough; this is the time to see the area. In the late fall, salmon run up the narrow stream, struggling against the fast current. With deer, elk and an occasional black bear, this area is alive with natural beauty and life. Banana slugs, beetles and pileated woodpeckers are also common sights, so keep your eyes peeled! However, even if you don't see any animals, this trail which used to be an old road is a perfect getaway year round.

LENA LAKE

Lena Lake

Nearest City: Hoodsport
Best Season: All
How Far: 5 Miles
Elevation Gain: 1300ft

Directions:
From Hoodsport travel
US 101 north for 14
miles. At milepost 318
turn left (west) onto
Hamma Hamma River
Road (Forest Road 25).
Continue for 7.5 paved
miles to the trailhead.

Don't be fooled by the rumors of crowds and poor conditions. Lena Lake is an awesome place. This trail is great for everyone, frequented by hikers of all ages and abilities. In fact, it is many hiker's first backpacking location. With a well-groomed trail full of switchbacks, bridges and tall trees, Lena Lake immediately takes you out of the city and into the wilds of the Olympic Peninsula.

Some claim this is quite a difficult trail, but all claim the reward (a large alpine lake cause by an earthquake hundreds of years ago) is worth it. It might not be the best alpine lake on the Olympic Peninsula, but with a paved road all the way to the trailhead, it is the best for accessibility.

Lena Lake, and the trail to the Brothers Base-camp is like stepping into the land of Narnia or into the Hobbit and Lord of the Rings. The Lena Lake Trail has giant, moss-covered boulders, snarled, giant cedar and fir trees and a lake that, on still days, reflects the neighboring hills perfectly. The trail also has one of the most picturesque wooden bridges on the Peninsula. Despite the fact that the creek is now underground, the raised wooden structure serves as a boundary. Crossing the bridge, you enter the wilderness of the Olympic Peninsula. This is a must hike for all.

STAIRCASE RAPIDS

Staircase Rapids

Nearest City: Hoodsport
Best Season: All
How Far: 4 Miles
Elevation Gain: 100ft

Directions: Hoodsport.
Turn left onto State Route
119 to a T intersection
with Forest Road 24.
Make a sharp left. In 1.7
miles the pavement ends.
Continue on a good
gravel road (FR 24) and
in 3.7 miles come to a
junction. Turn right and
drive 1.2 miles to the
Staircase Ranger Station.

Tucked away in the often forgotten Southeast side of the Olympic National Park, Staircase Rapids Loop trail is an excellent year round hike for the entire family. This loop, now completed with a new bridge, offers a leisurely walk along the Skokomish River.

In the summer, dip your feet in the cool waters running down the slopes of the Olympic Mountains. Walking under the canopy of cedar and fir trees that tower above you, Staircase gives you a walk that (like most of the Olympic Peninsula) is timeless. Staircase is a great hike for beginners and out of town guests.

Staircase Loop Trail is just one of the many experience in the Staircase region, but is a great warm up to a longer hike, or a great family picnic outing. The new bridge really makes the trail complete. After walking around this area, you will want to experience more of the Olympic National Park. If you want to start hiking, or just have an easy day where you take amazing pictures, this trail is for you. Some of my best memories are from this trail, especially snowshoeing in the winter. Check it out today!

MODERATE HIKES

The following hikes are difficult to some, easy to others. The incline might be tough, but most of these have views that will leave you speechless.

This section of moderate hikes are for those looking for a bit of a challenge without having to put on serious miles or insane elevation gain.

Be aware that in the winter, many of these trails will be snow-covered, making these awesome places to snowshoe. Year-round hiking can and should be done on all of these locations.

2ND BEACH, LAPUSH

2nd Beach LaPush

Nearest City: Forks
Best Season: All
How Far: 3.5 Miles
Elevation Gain: 200ft

Directions: From Forks, head North on Highway 101 for 1.5 miles. Turn left on Highway 110, stay to the left, heading to LaPush. .5 miles before the city of LaPush, the trailhead will be on your left.

While many people have a favorite beach along the Olympic Peninsula Coast, it is hard to beat the beauty that the trail and beach at 2nd Beach in the Quileute Nation. With a two-mile hike through a fantastically-groomed, densely-forested trail and a beach with sea stacks and tide pools filled with sea life, LaPush's 2nd Beach is a personal favorite.

There are few people who use this trail outside of the summer months, so this should be a destination when you want to have a beautiful, rocky beach to yourself. This is a stunning location; and during sunsets, there might not be a better place in the world. With pinks and reds and purples nearly every night, taking in a sunset here should be on everyone's bucket list. Even if you are here during the daytime, this place is fantastic. During storms or clear days, 2nd Beach will give you more reasons to fall in love with the beaches of Washington State.

This is not a beach in Oregon. Our beaches live up to the expectations. This beach and trail is family-friendly, and a perfect place for lunch. With over a mile of beach to explore, even if you aren't alone, finding a remote place is not difficult. 2nd Beach has beauty, views, solitude and the amazing arch at Teahwhit Head. If you are wanting one of the best beach experiences on the Washington Coast, the trail and the beach of 2nd Beach is what you crave.

SOUTH FORK OF THE HOH RIVER

South Fork of the Hoh River

Nearest City: Forks
Best Season: Summer/Fall
How Far: 6 Miles
Elevation Gain: 200ft

Directions:
From Forks travel south on US 101 for 14.5 miles. Turn left onto the Clearwater Road at milepost 176. Proceed on this paved road for 6.9 miles to a junction. Turn left onto Owl Creek Road. Bear right onto Maple Creek Road, following signs for the campground. After 5.4 miles cross the river and pass the campground Continue for another 2.3 miles, bearing right at an unmarked junction. In 0.5 mile the road ends at the trailhead.

Millions of visitors love the Hoh Rainforest, and the throngs of cars and tour buses drop countless visitors along the Hall of Mosses Trail and The Hoh River Trail. Luckily, there is a way to experience the Hoh Rainforest in near solitude. The South Fork of the Hoh River offers impressive views of the Hoh River, Hoh Peak and huge old growth and ancient forests.

The area is best-known for black bears, elk herds and salmon runs, making this an ideal place to be in the fall, as bears fish for salmon and the bugles of elk can be heard echoing off the hills. The well-maintained, barely-used trail is lined with neck high ferns, huge Douglas fir trees and gigantic Cedars, making the walk along this pristine section of wilderness one of the most relaxing and calming hikes on the Olympic Peninsula.

The trail can be walked for as long as you want, with conditions getting more difficult once you go 4 miles upstream. The best views of Hoh peak are about 3 miles in, and the best forests are a little over 2 miles, so hiking longer will reward you with better views. Plus, the farther you get from the car, the deeper into the magical Hoh wilderness you will get. Be constantly aware of bears, but don't let their presence in the region scare you away. The South Fork of the Hoh River truly is one of the Olympic National Park's best secret trails.

MOUNT ZION

Mount Zion

Nearest City: Quilcene
Best Season: Summer/Fall
How Far: 4.5 Miles
Elevation Gain: 1300ft

Directions:
From Quilcene, drive US 101 north. Turn left onto Lords Lake Loop Road. Turn left at a junction at Lords Lake. Continue and enter the Olympic National Forest. Bear right on gravel Forest Road 28 and climb 4.75 miles to an unmarked junction at Bon Jon Pass (pass the junction with FR 27). Bear right on FR 2810 and in 2.3 miles come to the Mount Zion trailhead.

Mount Zion is one of the many mountains that locals see often, but climb and hike rarely. The trail is perfect, the elevation gain is very tolerable and the views of Seattle, Mount Rainier and the rest of the Puget Sound are incredible. However, this isn't the only reason you should hike this trail. Usually in June, the well-maintained trail becomes more like a fireworks show than a hike, with thousands of rhododendrons blooming.

Hiking through an old fire area, flowers will bloom as you gain elevation toward the top of this rocky-summit mountain. Switchbacks are used, but none of them are too steep or too long, so hang in there. On a side note, if you love geology, the trail offers a few ledges made of basalt that are quite interesting. Overall, this is a good half-day hike. The trail is only 1.8 miles to the top, so if something looks interesting, stop and investigate.

Once at the top, the summit is craggy and rocky, but has a few areas that are flat. The summit used to house a fire lookout, but it has been gone for decades. The view used to be better,before the tree regrew from fires. Luckily, view-seeking hikers have made a new trail just to the southwest of the summit. Just a half-mile away, a fantastic view emerges from a rocky outcropping. This is where you should have lunch, take in the view and enjoy the foothills of the mighty Olympic Mountains.

5 MILE ISLAND

5 Mile Island

Nearest City: Forks
Best Season: All
How Far: 10 Miles
Elevation Gain 200ft

Directions:
From Forks travel south on US 101 for 12 miles to the Upper Hoh Road. (From Kalaloch head north on US 101 for 20 miles.) Head left (east) on the Upper Hoh Road for 18 miles to its end at a large parking lot, visitors center, and trailhead.

The Hoh Rainforest, the most famous temperate rainforest in the United States is so gorgeous it is hard to recommend just one trail. However, for the best experience, skip the Hall of Mosses trail and head down the Hoh River Trail to 5 Mile Island. This trail gives you the best rainforest experience, while not being stuck within a quarter mile of the visitor center. The Hoh Rainforest brings visitors from a round the world, but few venture down the river along this trail.

The trail to 5 Mile island, named because it is about 5 miles from the visitor center, is mostly flat, but lined with giant cedars, spruce, fir trees and endless ferns. With wooden bridges, streams and the occasional view of the mountains leading to Mount Olympus, this walk becomes a step back in time. With each mile behind you, you get deeper and deeper into the wilderness, with moss-covered trees shielding the sun or rain from you. At about four miles in, the trail becomes even better, with giant cedars lining the trail, the majority of which are hundreds of years old.

Elk herds visit these trails often in the early summer and late fall. Salmon, eagles and an occasional black bear may also be visible. However, the trail is best done if you are expecting a walk in the lush rainforest of the Olympic National Park. Since the trail is flat, it can be done by all levels of hikers and is a perfect introduction to longer hikes. If you want to see an old shelter, hike a half mile further to see the Happy Four Shelter, one of many emergency shelters on the Olympic Peninsula.

ELIP CREEK

Elip Creek

Nearest City: Aberdeen
Best Season: All
How Far: 14 Miles
Elevation Gain: 300ft

Directions:
Head North from
Aberdeen on Highway
101 toward Lake
Quinault. At South Shore
Road, take a right and
follow the road until you
reach a bridge that
crosses the river. Stay to
the right after the bridge
and follow the road until
the end. Trailhead is at
the end of the road.

A walk through the Quinault Rainforest is like nothing else on earth. While the crowds and infrastructure of the Olympic National Park tend to focus on the Hoh River Valley, the North Fork of the Quinault River is where some of the best sights are found. Huge cedars, gorgeous streams and a river stock full of salmon, with bears and eagles on the banks make this hike truly a local secret.

Mostly flat, the trail is well-maintained, aside from a few areas where wading across a shallow stream might be needed. Just pack a spare pair of shoes or sandals, wade through and continue down through giant ferns, moss-covered trees and some of the most relaxing spots by a river on the Peninsula. In the fall, salmon return upstream every year to spawn, and thanks to limited human use, bears and eagles are abundant. Once you reach Elip Creek, fording the river may not be possible, but enjoy the banks of the creek and take some time to explore downstream toward the Quinault.

The trail to Elip Creek is all about "being one with nature" and seeing the sheer power of the Olympic Peninsula. Used as a route during the first mapping expedition, also known as the Press Expedition of 1890, it is easy to see why this area become a favorite of all. Hiking here is both beautiful and historical, as the trail was also a common hunting trail for the Quinault tribe. Best seen during the summer and fall months, this section can be hiked year-round, and should be hiked often.

BLUE MOUNTAIN

Blue Mountain

Nearest City: Sequim
Best Season: Summer
How Far: 1 Mile
Elevation Gain170ft

Directions:
Headed west on Hwy 101 towards Port Angeles, turn left at Deer Park Rd. Travel along the paved road, and continue along the dirt road. Once you reach the dirt road, you will be within the National Park boundaries. It is 18 miles from Hwy 101 to the trailhead.

With over four times less precipitation than falls on the summit of Mount Olympus, it is hard to understand why Blue Mountain isn't one of the most talked about ridge views in the state. While it is more remote than Hurricane Ridge, thanks to an unpaved road, the trail, leading to amazing views, is only half a mile. However, one can walk for hours along the ridges in either direction, making this a local favorite.

The trail to the mountain is called the Rainshadow Nature Trail, and it lives up to the title. Typically, when rain is dumping on the westside of the Olympics, this trail is either dry or has light mist coming down. The entire area averages only 50 inches of precipitation a year, making this trail a well-deserved destination during the rainy months. Sadly, the road is closed once the snow comes, so this isn't a year round hike unless you want to walk along the road for an extra nine miles.

The ridges along Blue Mountain show the folds and creases of the Olympic Mountain Range, a great example of plate tectonics. With views of Mount Baker, Vancouver Island and the entire Olympic interior, it is hard not to want to just sit in one place and take in the views. Do, however, explore the ridges and see marmots, deer, rabbits and hawks. Blue Mountain is the perfect hike for little effort, amazing views and solitude.

LAKE ANGELES

Lake Angeles

Nearest City: Port
Angeles
Best Season: All
How Far: 7.4 Miles
Elevation Gain: 2400ft

Directions:
From Port Angeles
leave US 101 to Race
Street south 1.2 miles
to Hurricane Ridge
Road (Heart o' the Hills
Parkway) Proceed on
Hurricane Ridge Road
for 5 miles. Just before
the park entrance
booth, turn right to
reach a large trailhead
parking area.

Like most awesome destinations on the Olympic Peninsula, the trail to Lake Angeles has quite the climb. With over 2,000 feet of elevation gain in the 3.8 miles to get to the lake, this hike is best done in the early morning or evening. However, even if you do find yourself on the trail at mid-day, the path is shady and cool. Located below Klahhane Ridge, the lake is beautiful, deep and refreshing: everything you want in a lake hike.

The lake, left-over from the days of glaciers, is surrounded on three sides by steep, craggy cliffs. A small island sits in the middle, begging those ready for an adventure to swim to her banks. Yes, this picturesque lake is deep enough for swimming; but more importantly, large enough to find a spot all to yourself. The trail and lake can get crowded, but don't worry: Lake Angeles is more of a local favorite than a tourist destination. Perfectly located, close to town, this is an ideal hike when there is a break in the weather.

For the best time at Lake Angeles, either go up in late spring as the snow melts around the lake, which sits at 4,000 ft or go up during the winter to see it as a snowy wonderland. The trail is also runnable for those who enjoy trail-running. For lakes in the Olympics, this should become a favorite. Seeing it on a hot day or with snow around the banks makes the incline well worth the effort.

GOBLIN'S GATE

Goblin's Gate

Nearest City: Port Angeles
Best Season: All
How Far: 2.4 Miles
Elevation Gain: 200ft

Directions:
Head West on Highway
101 for 8 miles. Take a left
on Olympic Hot Springs
Road. Turn left of Whiskey
Bend Road and follow
road to completion.

The Elwha River should be the most famous river in the world. Having two dams removed and having salmon return to it for the first time in 100 years, the Elwha River also offers some gorgeous sights. Goblin's Gate, an awesomely named gorge, is a sight that needs to be seen more.

As the old-growth flanked Elwha winds down to the Straight of Juan de Fuca, it takes a sharp turn through Goblin's Gate. No more than maybe two hundred feet tall, Goblin's Gate comes out of nowhere, forming a narrow passage for the river to flow through. With blue and gray water foaming below, the trail to this spot is as beautiful as the mouth of Goblin's Gate.

The trail along the Elwha River weaves through a forest that could have inspired Grimm. Trees line the trail, as do huge ferns and downed wooden giants. At the right time of the day, mist raises up from the ground and clouds meet the tops of the trees, giving the forest a mystical light. The trail, occasionally covered in reddish cedar dust, is well-taken care of and great for hikers of all ages.

MOUNT WALKER

Mount Walker

Nearest City: Quilcene
Best Season: All
How Far: .5 to 5 Miles
Elevation Gain: 0 to
2000ft

Directions:
From Quilcene drive
US 101 south for 5
miles. Just north of
milepost 300, turn left
onto Mount Walker
Road (Forest Service
2730) and proceed
0.25 mile to the
trailhead. When the
road is closed, park at
the gate.

Straight up to a tree-lined mountain top, a few thousand feet above sea-level, the Mount Walker trail rises and circles a cone shaped mountain near the mouth of the Hood Canal. This sounds super rad, and it is, because of the two great views. With a panoramic view of the Salish Sea and the Puget Sound on one side, and a wall-poster-quality view of the Olympic Mountains at the other, the sights from this mountain are awesome.

With two unique views, there are two ways up to the top of this mountain. One is a half-day long hike that zigs and zags up the mountain in a great display of the Olympic Peninsula's forests. The other is by car, up a dirt road that comically circles the small mountain. Both ways are great, and depending on your mood, and the time of the year, you have options. The road is only open when there is no snow, so it is closed all winter long. The trail is open year round and is typically used only by locals for a great snowshoeing day. In the summer, the road is well-used, as is the trail.

On a clear day, your eyes will rest on the glacier-filled peaks of Mount Rainier, then fall to the city of Seattle, with the ferry visible, ever so small. Even on a cloudy day, timed just-right, you can emerge at the top in the sun, seeing nothing but a few tops of Douglas Fir trees and a sea of clouds below your feet. The views aren't just of the city. Looking west, you can see the craggy peaks of the Olympics standing guard over the rainforests. Even this can be improved upon. If you want this to be heart-stopping, go here at sunset.

BIG CREEK

Big Creek

Nearest City: Hoodsport
Best Season: All
How Far: 4.5 Miles
Elevation Gain: 1000ft

Directions:
From Shelton travel north on US 101 to Hoodsport. Turn left onto State Route 119 to a T intersection with Forest Road 24. Make a sharp left and immediately turn right into the Big Creek Campground. The trailhead is located near the picnic shelter.

Finding a hike that is accessible year-round can be a challenge, but the Big Creek Trail offers much more than is known to most non-locals. With a great loop through cascading creeks and small moss-banked waterfalls, this trail fails to disappoint year-round. With a connecting trail to Mount Ellinor, you can choose just how impressive of a day you want.

The Big Creek loop is best taken clockwise, to make the down climb less steep, but that means the uphill sections can get a little rough. Don't let that stop you, though. As this trail offers some of the more accessible, scenic wooden bridges on the entire Olympic Peninsula. With water flowing below you, sit atop the many rocks near the creek and enjoy a snack or a nap. On hot days, take a dip, soak your feet and enjoy the cool waters running off from Mount Ellinor and Mount Washington.

The Big Creek Trail is not too difficult, very accessible and well-marked. On hot summer days, it can be crowded by Olympic Peninsula standards but is always worth the effort. The trail is shaded and has benches to rest on, so this is a hike most hikers can complete. Our personal favorite time to hike this trail is a warm early Spring day. You will more than likely have the trail to yourself, and the fresh runoff will have the waterfalls and streams flowing like crazy.

SHI SHI BEACH

Shi Shi Beach

Nearest City: Port Angeles
Best Season: All
How Far: 8 Miles
Elevation Gain: 200ft

Directions: From Port Angeles follow US 101 to SR 112, to Neah bay. Follow the brown signs for "Cape Flattery". Turn left on Fort Street for one block, then right on 3rd Street (unmarked). In another block (0.1 mile), turn left on Cape Flattery Road. (Follow this road 2.5 miles, then turn left over the bridge onto Hobuck Road. Staying on the main paved road, follow signs for the fish hatchery. Drive to the parking lot at the trailhead, located on your right.

Trails don't get much more remote than Shi Shi beach along the Olympic Peninsula Coast; but what it lacks in convenience, it makes up for in sheer, rugged beauty. The coast areas in the Olympic National Park receive over a hundred inches of rain each year, and storms packing giant waves and 60 miles an hour winds are common in the winter months. Yet, Shi Shi beach, year-in-and-out remains one of the most beautiful beaches in the State of Washington.

Located near Neah Bay, the beaches out here offer hours of exploration in tide pools, filled with numerous sea creatures, set below sea stacks. There might not be a better place to spend a hot summer day or during a wet, rainy storm than Shi Shi Beach. Visitors to this area often have a hard time returning to their cities because of the beauty. The best trail is heading toward Point of Arches, but be aware that the first 1.75 miles are through thick spruce forests. After you reach the National Park, climb down a bluff and you are on the beach.

Watch for whales, seals, and bald eagles. Reaching the sea stacks is an eight mile round-trip hike, but the feeling one gets from seeing Point of Arches is indescribable. For the best experience at Shi Shi beach, you should see it twice: once in the summer sun and again during a winter storm. Yes, it rains a lot here, but nothing makes this beach more impressive than to see it during the "highs" and "lows" of weather.

MARMOT PASS

Marmot Pass

Nearest City: Quilcene
Best Season: Summer/
Fall
How Far: 10.5 Miles
Elevation Gain: 3500ft

Directions: From
Quilcene drive US 101
south for 1.5 miles.
Turn right onto Penny
Creek Road. After 1.5
miles bear left onto Big
Quilcene River Road
(Forest Road 27). Drive
9.25 miles, turning left
on FR 2750. Continue
4.75 miles to the
trailhead.

Marmot Pass stands at 6,000 feet, but the elevation isn't the draw. The trail and the journey make the 3500 feet climb over 5.3 miles each way seem like a breeze to most conditioned day-hikers. With views of the interior of the Olympic Mountains and the Puget Sound, it is easy to see why this is an incredibly popular trail year-round. While typically done as a day hike, we recommend using this as a jumping off point for an overnight or multi-night hike.

Hiking up the Quilcene River, experience everything from old-growth forests to wildflower fields before you get to the dusty, dry summit. Along the way, pass by campgrounds and keep your eyes open for deer, black bear and of course, marmots. Mountain goats can also be seen, but keep your distance, as they are known to be quite aggressive.

Marmot Pass is a perfect hike for those who enjoy big views, elevation gain and an incredible photo opportunity. While the route in the winter can be a bit dicey because of snow and wind, the solitude during the winter months makes the views even that much better. Bring binoculars, scan for animals or just sit back and watch ships sail along Hood Canal and the Puget Sound.

MOUNT TOWNSEND

Mount Townsend

Nearest City: Quilcene
Best Season: Summer/
Fall
How Far: 8.2 Miles
Elevation Gain: 3000ft

Directions:
From Quilcene drive US
101 south for 1.5 miles.
Turn right onto Penny
Creek Road. After 1.5
miles bear left onto Big
Quilcene River Road
(Forest Road 27). Drive
13.5 miles, ignoring the
sign at 12.5 miles for
the Mount Townsend
Trail. Turn left onto FR
27-190 and in 0.75 mile
come to the trailhead.

With views of Seattle, Sequim, Port Angeles, and both the Cascade and Olympic Mountain Ranges, it is hard to find a more accessible mountain to climb than Mount Townsend. Standing just above 6,000ft, this tree-free mountain is everything you would expect from a mountain on the northeast corner of the Olympic Peninsula. With over 30 switchbacks and varying terrain, this is a trail for hikers of nearly all abilities.

On this trail, the well-groomed path meanders back and forth, rising from old growth forests with rhododendrons to wildflower-filled meadows until you eventually reach the ridge-line of the mountain. Take your time as you are heading up. If the weather is clear, Seattle, Mount Rainier and the Hood Canal Bridge can be visible to the east. Once you reach the saddle, take a break and enjoy the fantastic views of the interior of the Olympic Mountain range. Don't just hang out here, though. Climb the ridge to the north and stand atop Mount Townsend.

Mount Townsend is a fantastic climb year-round, but be aware that it is quite steep and water is limited on the trail. Despite the elevation gain, this is a good all-season trail, and hiking to the top should be done a few times a year. For an added bonus, climb up here on the 4th of July and watch the fireworks erupt across Puget Sound and the Salish Sea.

TUBAL
CAIN

Exotic Hikes

Tubal Cain/Tull Canyon

Nearest City: Sequim
Best Season: Spring/
Summer
How Far: 8 Miles
Elevation Gain: 1400ft

Directions:
From Sequim, head East on
Highway 101. Turn onto
Louella Road. Turn left on
Palo Alto Road. Bear right
at a junction onto Forest
Road 2880. Turn left on FR
2870. In 2.6 miles bear
right at a junction to
continue on FR 2870
(formerly called FR 2860).
Continue 10 miles to the
trailhead.

Nearly 22 miles Southeast of Sequim, one doesn't immediately think of awe-someness. Don't get me wrong, the area is beautiful; but it is so remote that I typically just glance out the car window as I fly by on my way to Hurricane Ridge, Dungeness Spit or Lake Crescent. However, if you take the time to stop off in the area, a very pleasant, gorgeous surprise will await you.

In mid-summer, this trail is like the 4th of July, with Rhododendrons blooming like fireworks in the sky. With reds and purples exploding through the layers of green, the body doesn't seem to mind the steady incline that this trail gives.

Once you arrive at the Tubal Cain Mine area, the trail basically disappears. You will know that you have arrived at this point because mine debris litters the area. With a campground located basically on the trail itself, and hundreds of camp-ers stomping down a path to everywhere, the trail becomes difficult to follow. To get to the Mine, stay on the left and you will see a large gravel deposit, with a horrible steep incline of scree. While it isn't advised to go into the mineshaft, take a few minutes and take some pictures from inside. Rarely can one find such a remote cave that is so intact.

For an added bonus, on the way back, head up the trail to the right, just a half mile from Tubal Cain. This leads up to Tull Canyon, where the remains of a min-ing town and a B-17 bomber still lay in the remote valley.

HURRICANE HILL

Hurricane Hill

Nearest City: Port Angeles
Best Season: Summer/
Winter
How Far: 3 Miles
Elevation Gain: 1000ft

Directions:
From Port Angeles leave
US 101 near milepost
249, following Race Street
south 1.2 miles to
Hurricane Ridge Road. In
the summer, drive 17.5
miles to the Hurricane
Ridge Visitors Center and
continue 1.5 miles farther
on the narrow Hurricane
Hill Road to trailhead
parking.

With views of the Olympic Mountains, Vancouver Island and Mount Baker, one could spend hours standing atop Hurricane Hill taking in the sights. Luckily, during the summer months, this trail is easy enough for the whole family to enjoy. In the winter, the trail is longer and covered in snow, but offering some of the best-groomed areas for snowshoeing and cross country skiing in the Olympic National Park.

Located just past the Hurricane Ridge Visitor Center, this trail is a year round favorite for tourists and locals alike. Chances are, you won't be alone on this trail, but there are plenty of places to take in a view in silence. Hurricane Hill can be steep to beginning hikers, but the reward is worth the effort.

During the late summer, marmots, deer and wildflowers are abundant, with an occasional mountain goat sighting possible on the nearby ridges. Hurricane Hill isn't the hardest hike, (not even close!) which is why the views it gives are even better. For minimal effort and maximum reward, on a clear day this hike is hard to beat.

DODGER POINT BRIDGE

Dodger Point Bridge

Nearest City: Port Angeles
Best Season: All
How Far: 7 Miles
Elevation Gain: 600ft

Directions:
Head West on Highway
101 for 8 miles. Take a left
on Olympic Hot Springs
Road. Turn left of Whiskey
Bend Road and follow road
to completion.

The Elwha River should be the most known river in the nation, as it is home to the largest dam removal operation in the world. The Elwha River is also home to the second largest environmental restoration in US history, making this area one of the few places where the impact of man is being reversed on a grand scale. For nearly one hundred years, two dams devastated the local environment and all but killed the salmon run. Now, with the removal of the dams, the river is back to her natural path, and wildlife is flocking back.

The trail to the bridge weaves through a well-groomed trail, past homestead areas and through ridiculously magical forests. While the forests of the Elwha aren't as grand in scale as the Hoh and Quinault regions, they are just as photogenic and visually pleasing. Once you reach the beautiful cable bridge, stand in the middle or along the banks of the Elwha river and take in the sheer power and scale. With a washout canyon area to the south and a fantastic river basin downstream to the north, the bridge is a perfect destination for a meal after a medium-day hike. On the return route, check out Goblin's Gate.

MOUNT ELLINOR

Mount Ellinor

Nearest City: Hoodsport
Best Season: Early Fall/
Winter
How Far: 3.2 Miles
Elevation Gain: 2300ft

Directions: From Shelton
travel north on US 101 to
Hoodsport. Turn left onto
State Route to a T
intersection with Forest
Road 24. Turn right onto
graveled FR 24. Turn left
onto FR 2419. Continuing
on FR 2419 for 1.6 miles,
come to a junction. Turn
left on FR 2419-014 and
follow it 1 mile to the
upper trailhead.

Hiking Mount Ellinor is almost a right of passage for mountain climbing on the Olympic Peninsula. While technically a mountain, in the summer months it is a steep hike that offers some of the best views of the Olympic Peninsula. At neatly 6,000 ft, on a sunny day one can see the city of Seattle, Mount Rainier, Mount Saint Helens, Mount Olympus, Lake Cushman and the Hood Canal.

From the upper parking lot, which is open from about June until early October, the trail is only 3.2 miles round trip, making it a perfect day hike. More than likely, you won't be the only one on the mountain; but once you see the view from the top, the elevation gain and the crowds just fade away. With eagles, hawks and the occasional mountain goat also visible, this trail might just become a favorite.

The Mount Ellinor Trail has snow on it from October to June. Late July, August and September are the best months for snow free hiking conditions. Winter makes the mountain difficult, but using crampons and an ice axe, the views and climb are fantastic.

COLONEL BOB PEAK

Colonel Bob

Nearest City:
Aberdeen
Best Season: Summer/
Fall
How Far: 8.2 Miles
Elevation Gain: 3200ft

Directions:
From Aberdeen travel
north on US 101. Just
past milepost 112 turn
right onto Donkey
Creek Road (Forest
Road 22) Follow this
paved road for 8 miles
to a junction. Turn left
onto FR 2204 and
continue 11 miles to the
trailhead at Petes
Creek.

Colonel Bob is a must-hike trail that offers truly breathtaking views of the Olympic Mountains, the Quinault Rainforest and Lake Quinault. On a clear day, this rugged peak is the perfect place to sit and watch the world below. High above the Quinault River Valley, it is easy to drift away to hundreds of years ago, as many of the sights you see are mostly unchanged.

This trail isn't easy, with large steps and rolling hills, but with high alpine fields reminiscent of The Sound of Music, the climb up to the top of this peak is worth the effort. While wildlife sightings are rare on this trail, an occasional black bear, deer or maybe elk could cross in front of you.

Colonel Bob is a hike that will be cemented in your memory forever. Sitting atop her rugged summit, the view below makes you feel alive, and the sights into the Olympic National Park interior will only make your desire to explore grow.

FLETCHER CANYON

Fletcher Canyon

Nearest City:
Aberdeen
Best Season: All
How Far: 4 Miles
Elevation Gain: 1000ft

Directions:
From Hoquiam travel
north on US 101. Turn
right onto the South
Shore Road. Proceed
on this road for 12
miles. The trail begins
at the end of a small
spur on the south side
of the road. If the spur
is flooded, park instead
on the north side of the
South Shore Road.

The Quinault Rainforest isn't as popular as the Hoh rainforest, but what it lacks in crowds, it makes up in sheer awesomeness. The trail to Fletcher Canyon is one of those trails that should be very popular but instead is forgotten about for more publicized areas. Fletcher Canyon is like walking back in a time machine, with each mile hiked pushing you until you are standing at the edge of a canyon that could be from the dawn of time.

Fletcher Canyon is a 4-mile round-trip hike that is harder than it should be, but completely worth the numerous creek crossings, steep inclines and loose gravel. Located in the Colonel Bob wilderness, sunlight nearly vanishes as the Fletcher Canyon canopy grows thicker and thicker. With ferns higher than your waist, the greens of this area are nearly impossible to replicate, but nature does a good job doing so. At about a mile in, the trail gets even better, even if the trail gets steeper. Moss-covered boulders and towering fir trees abound, making the views of the canyon even more spectacular.

Toward the end of the trail, the path crosses a log that offers a pristine view of the creek and canyon. Eat a lunch here, sit back and relax and know that you are one of the few people to gaze upon this wonderful, remote canyon. Fletcher Canyon is the perfect trail to get away from the hustle and bustle of the city, and it is the perfect trail to step back into time and see the Olympic Peninsula the way it has always been.

ADVANCED HIKES

The following hikes are difficult. The incline is usually quite insane and the milage is long. You will sweat on nearly all of these hikes, but the reward is some of the most impressive destinations in the world.

Advanced hikers should be able to walk upwards of 10 miles a day and be fine with steep inclines, rough trails and route finding.

In the winter, the majority of these trails will be in rough condition. Be aware that these all can be quite dangerous and must only be attempted by serious hikers.

ELWHA RIVER TO HURRICANE HILL

Elwha to Hurricane Hill

Nearest City: Port Angeles
Best Season: Summer/Fall
How Far: 12.2 Miles
Elevation Gain: 5000ft

Directions:
Head West on Highway 101 for 8 miles. Take a left on Olympic Hot Springs Road. Turn left of Whiskey Bend Road and follow road to completion.

Hiking in the Olympic National Park, one can experience numerous ecosystems on just one trail, and the trail leading from the Whiskey Bend area of the Elwha River leading up to Hurricane Ridge might just be the best example. With the trail leading you from near sea level to high atop the Olympic Range, strong quads and calves are a must. This can be a tiring hike, but the sights one sees on the numerous switchbacks and ridge-lines make this a must-hike trail.

The trail weaves up the mountains, allowing you to experience dense forests, sub-alpine meadows and fantastic views from barren ridges. With a well-maintained path that is used less than it should be, the route to Hurricane Hill will tire you out. It makes no promises or allusion to easiness; but with ever-increasing views, you won't feel the tiredness in your lungs and legs. The trail is also part of the Pacific Northwest trail, so seeing an occasional rugged hiker may happen. Bears, deer and marmots may also be seen, with mountain goats sparsely populating the nearby peaks.

From the Elwha River Trailhead, the trail does not go downhill. This is all uphill, and for the first four miles, you get to hike in a cool, tree-covered canopy. After four miles, you break out of the forests and continue up more switchbacks, but now with a great view. The views are the destination, but the route up will make you even more thankful while you take in the sights of the Olympic Mountains, the Straight of Juan de Fuca and Vancouver Island.

FLAPJACK LAKES

Flapjacks Lake

Nearest City:
Hoodsport
Best Season: Summer/
Fall
How Far: 15 Miles
Elevation Gain: 3000ft

Directions:
From Shelton travel
north on US 101 for 15
miles to Hoodsport.
Turn left onto State
Route 119 to a T
intersection with Forest
Road 24. Make a
sharp left. In 1.7 miles
the pavement ends.
Continue on a good
gravel road (FR 24)
and in 3.7 miles come
to a junction. Turn right
and drive 1.2 miles to
the Staircase Ranger
Station.

High alpine lakes are hit and miss in the Olympic National Park, but Flapjack Lakes is a destination that needs to be reached. With a mostly gentle climb and fantastic trails, the hike here feels more like walking along an old road, which in some places you are. The route follows the route taken by the 1890 O'Neil Expedition, which helped map the entire region.

The trail along the North Fork of the Skokomish River weaves up through cedars and maple trees, passing the now-rebuilt Staircase Rapids Bridge. With areas to stop and take in the sights, this hike should be done leisurely, as it will take most of the day anyway. Generally, the trail is simple to follow with only one fork in the way. A little over three miles in, you will come to the Flapjack Lakes junction at Spike Camp. Follow the signs and stick to the right, which slowly climbs up for the next four miles. Be aware that the trail does get steeper after you reach an area known as Donahue Creek, but will let up when you get to a side junction to Smith and Black and White Lakes. Past this junction, you only have about a half mile until you reach the fantastic lakes.

Flapjack Lakes are smallish lakes, but are gorgeous due to the fact that the views of the little-talked about Sawtooth Range of the Olympics is seen. The views, during the right lighting and seasons can be breathtaking. If you are lucky, the wind will be calm, the bugs will be low, and you will be able to see a perfect reflection of of these seasonally-popular lakes.

MOUNT BALDY

Mount Baldy

Nearest City: Sequim
Best Season: Summer/Fall
How Far: 7 Miles
Elevation Gain: 4,000ft

Directions:
Take Palo Alto road off of Hwy 101, east of Sequim. Drive to the end of the paved road, then turn right on forest service gravel road 2880. Continue straight (#2870) and hit junction with road #2860 at 12 miles, coming in from your left. Stay right and continue up. Come to a sign with says "Upper Dungeness Trail 2 miles". There is an unmarked road going right. Turn right and drive 1.7 miles to the end of the old fire road.

If you are a fan of ridge-line climbs on the more dry corner of the Olympic Peninsula, the hike to Mount Baldy is one of the classics. Rising up to 6500 ft, the views are stunning, the climb is steep and the experience is one of the hikes you dream about. With wildflowers in mid-summer and the occasional mountain goat year-round, this hike is not only beautiful, but you may just be the only person on the trail. If you love solitude on ridges and meadows that belong in the Sound of Music, this trail needs to be hiked.

The trail itself steadily climbs, with sections of scree that can pose a threat to your ankles. Don't worry, it is worth it. While the trail is in the more dry section of the Olympic Peninsula, snow can be present from October to June. The ridge-line hike is great all year, and at 9 miles round trip, it makes for a great day-hike. With an elevation gain of 3700 ft, be prepared to pace yourself and bring plenty of water.

The best route for the trail is to start near the Maynard Burn, which signs along the road will lead you to. Once on the trail, watch for signs that tell you about the Tyler Peak Trail which is to the right. This trail is less steep and was created by hunters, so the boot path is pretty well used. The trail will soon become wide open, offering views of lush meadows and ridges. Be aware of the false summit, though! You will need navigation skills. A topo map or GPS will really help you not get lost if and when clouds roll in and block your view.

CUB PEAK

Cub Peak

Nearest City: Hoodsport
Best Season: Summer/
Fall
How Far: 6.6 Miles
Elevation Gain: 4000ft

Directions:
From Shelton travel north
on US 101 for 15 miles to
Hoodsport. Turn left onto
State Route 119 to a T
intersection with Forest
Road 24. Make a sharp
left. In 1.7 miles the
pavement ends. Continue
on a good gravel road
(FR 24) and in 3.7 miles
come to a junction. Turn
right and drive 1.2 miles
to the Staircase Ranger
Station.

A rugged peak exists in the Southeast corner of the Olympic National Park where few hikers venture to go. The top is ragged in places, with exposed rocks teetering precariously at the top of a 3,000 ft drop. Away from the danger, clay, shale and ballast mix together around breathtaking wildflowers and viewpoints of the Skokomish River Valley, the Hamma Hamma River Valley, The Brothers, Mount Constance, Mount Ellinor and Mount Washington. The highlight, though, might just be the aptly-named Sawtooth Range, standing over the Skokomish River Valley and forest, jagged edges of a logging tool that was spared for this forest. The mountains are magnificent, the wildflowers are beautiful and the view is almost as breathtaking as the trail to get here.

The route to Cub Peak in the Olympic National Park nearly gives you the entire Olympic National Park rolled into one hike. Starting along the Skokomish River, the trail climbs through dark green, old, dense ferns and forests before going to a High Alpine Lake (Wagon Wheel Lake) surrounded by high cliffs, rounded peaks, rhododendrons and tall trees. To the left of the lake, a small trail that looks more like an animal trails climbs sharply up. Climb up through this scree, you soon reach a small plateau and ridge, full of wildflowers, giving you a panoramic view few have seen. Cub Peak is an amazing hike. It is steep and not for beginning climbers, but should be attempted at some point in your life. Climb it and tell me that it isn't one of the more awesome mountains close to Olympia. That is, after you ice your legs.

HOH LAKE

Hoh Lake

Nearest City: Port Angeles
Best Season: Summer/ Fall
How Far: 19.5 Miles
Elevation Gain: 2800ft

Directions: From Port Angeles follow US 101. Turn left onto the Sol Duc Hot Springs Road. Follow this road for 12 miles. Just past the Eagle Ranger Station turn right into the Sol Duc Hot Springs Resort.

If you love hiking miles for a small alpine lake with great views, the way to Hoh Lake may just become a favorite. With elk and bear usually seen in the summer and early fall months, and wildflowers lasting until October, the trek to Hoh Lake is well worth the miles on your legs. This is for advanced hikers and should be a goal for any moderate hiker.

With two routes, you have your choice of just how difficult you want this hike to be. From The Hoh River trail, it is over 28 miles round trip, but the sights you see make this marathon-like hike extremely worth it. From the Hoh Visitor Center, the trail meanders along the Hoh River until it sharply climbs 3,000 feet over 22 switchbacks. The word exhausting comes closest to describing the route. The lake is gorgeous, but only experienced hikers looking for an insane day should go this way. Instead, start from Sol Duc and make the trail, which is only 19.5 miles. It is a steep climb too, but the route out to Hoh Lake, and to say you hiked here in a day will make the blisters worth it.

The experience and views are the reasons you should hike this trail. The trail is in fantastic shape and well used, making it an ideal trail run or speed hike. The lake, situated in a basin between snow-capped peaks isn't insanely gorgeous, but views of the rainforest, the Olympic Mountains and the animals along the way are. With old growth, ridges, waterfalls and rivers to see, making this a 2-day or 3-day trip could have you falling in love with backpacking in the Olympic National Park.

COPPER MOUNTAIN

Copper Mountain

Nearest City: Hoodsport
Best Season: Summer/
Fall
How Far: 7.5 Miles
Elevation Gain: 4500ft

Directions:
From Shelton travel north
on US 101 to Hoodsport.
Turn left onto State Route
119 to a T intersection
with Forest Road 24.
Make a sharp left. In 1.7
miles the pavement ends.
Continue on a good
gravel road (FR 24) and
in 3.7 miles come to a
junction. Turn right and
drive 1.2 miles to the
Staircase Ranger Station.

If you are looking for a leg-burning hike that is one of the steepest in the Olympic National Park, Copper Mountain is for you. Located above the rough Wagonwheel Lake trail, the Copper Mountain Trail rises quickly to the right of the lake. With nothing more than what first starts out as an animal path, you quickly rise above the trees and onto a craggy summit that offers amazing views of the Hood Canal Region, the interior of the Olympic Mountains (including a great view of Mount Ellinor) and the Skokomish River Valley.

With an elevation gain of 4400 ft over 5 miles, this isn't for inexperienced hikers. Route-finding skills are needed, and bringing a detailed map along is recommended. The trail branches up to the south of Wagonwheel Lake and snakes along the ridge-line to the top of the mountain. With Mountain goats and an occasional bear around, you might catch some wildlife, but don't expect to see another person. This is a mountain that is climbed just a few times a week at best, so do some extra research on the area before hand.

This trail should be done when you need something tough and and to push beyond your limits. Like most hard hikes, the view is worth the difficulty. Standing atop this little-known, often-seen and rarely-climbed mountain, you get a good idea just how immense the wilderness of the Olympic National Park can be.

7 LAKES BASIN

7 Lakes Basin

Nearest City: Port Angeles
Best Season: Summer/Fall
How Far: 19 Miles
Elevation Gain: 4,000ft

Directions:
From Port Angeles follow US 101 west. Turn left onto the Sol Duc Hot Springs Road. Follow this road for 12 miles. Pass the Eagle Ranger Station and turn right into the Sol Duc Hot Springs Resort.

Considered by many to be the best long-day hike in the Olympic Peninsula, this Sol Duc hike offers the widest variety of sights and animals in the park. With bear, elk, marmots and mountain goats often seen on or near the trail, animals lovers will enjoy this trail. If you like vistas, ridges, waterfalls and lakes, this trail also has you covered, giving you some of the most spectacular views of Mount Olympus and the Bailey Range from the trail. If you are looking for the one trail that has it all, this might just be it! The only downside is it is 19 miles long, so prepare for a long day of beauty.

Starting at Sol Duc, the trail is marked as the 7-Lakes Basin. You have a choice right away. Bear to the left and meander along the Sol Duc River, or stick to the right and climb up right away. Either way, you will have over 4,000 ft of elevation gain. Locals prefer sticking to the right, following the trail up to Canyon Creek Falls then hitting the trail to the aptly-named Deer Lake. Following the path toward Hoh Lake, you soon get rewarded with amazing views of the entire Hoh River Valley and Mount Olympus. Stick to the High Divide Trail, and the 7 Lakes Basin becomes visible before you return back on the Sol Duc trail

With many lakes and a few trails, this is an epic hike that is far too amazing to describe in a few paragraphs. In short, this trail has it all. Make sure you follow the route well, as to not get lost. It is recommended that you bring along a map of the area and familiarize yourself with the route before you head out.

MOUNT STORM KING

Mount Storm King

Nearest City: Port Angeles
Best Season: Year Round
How Far: 3.8 Miles
Elevation Gain: 1700ft

Directions:
From Port Angeles follow US 101 west for 20 miles to Barnes Point at milepost 228 and turn right. In 0.2 mile, at a stop sign, turn right and proceed to a large parking area. The trail begins on the Marymere Falls Nature Trail near the rustic Storm King Ranger Station.

If the words "Danger: Exposed Ledges" excite you on a hike, Mount Storm King is a great trail for you. If those words scare you, you should still try Mount Storm King. Located only 2,400 feet above sea level and 1700 ft above Lake Crescent, this trail can be quite the popular draw. Sharing a route with the well-travelled Marymere Falls Trail, the Storm King trail darts off to the left and quickly up the mountain after a well-placed, somewhat ominous-looking sign.

At 3.8 miles round-trip with only 1700 ft of elevation gain, this route is a great day-hike and another spot to have a great lunch with a view. While the view isn't as grand as some other mountains, the fact that you get to sit high above unsuspecting cars on Highway 101 and hundreds of tourists along Lake Crescent is worth the trek up. With views of lush forested valleys and the gorgeous Lake Crescent, it is easy to see why warnings about exposed ledges are needed.

With the majority of the trail under an old growth forest, and within walking distance to theLake and Marymere Falls, Mount Storm King makes for a great 3-part day. Climb the mountain in the morning, take in the falls after lunch, and enjoy a sunset on Lake Crescent, knowing that you have experienced some of the best easy access trails in the area.

LAKE CONSTANCE

Lake Constance

Nearest City: Quilcene
Best Season: Summer/
Fall
How Far: 13 Miles
(Approx)
Elevation Gain: 3300ft

Directions:
From Quilcene follow
US 101 south 11 miles
to Brinnon. Turn right
on Dosewallips Road
and drive 8.7 miles.

Lake Constance is the steepest hike in the Olympic National Park. With little more than an animal trail, thanks to a forest fire that burnt through the area, sections of this hike seem like they would be easier on your hands and knees. It sounds hard, and it is, but like most difficult hikes, the risk and effort fades away when you are standing on the pretty, mountain-encircled shores of Lake Constance.

The lake is on the smallish side and appears even smaller next to the amazingly huge peaks of Mount Constance and C-141 peak rising from the shores. With frequent mountain goat sightings and few people sightings, this trail is a nature lover's ideal area. Despite the struggles getting to the lake, it is also a perfect place to star gaze or prepare for a climb of some of the most difficult mountains on the Olympic Peninsula.

Lake Constance is not for everyone; in fact, some would argue it isn't for anyone. Those people would be wrong, though. After a few minutes of catching your breath, the view behind you, looking at The Brothers, and the view in front of you will re-energize you, allowing you to properly appreciate the gorgeousness of the area.

PYRAMID PEAK

Pyramid Peak

Nearest City: Port Angeles
Best Season: All
How Far: 7 Miles
Elevation Gain: 2500ft

Directions:
From Port Angeles follow US 101 west for 27 miles. Turn right on Camp David Jr. Road (aka North Shore Road) and proceed for 3.2 miles to a small pullout adjacent to the North Shore Picnic Area. The trail begins on the opposite side of the road.

Few things are better than standing atop a mountain, looking down on a beautiful lake. Throw in a cabin that was used during WWII and views of the Olympic Mountains and the Elwha River Valley and you have Pyramid Peak. Standing nearly 2500ft above Lake Crescent, this is the ideal place to go on a clear day.

While hiking the trail, be aware that a big slide recently occurred, making the trail EXTREMELY narrow in places at the 1.75 mile mark. After this sketchy part in the trail, it widens back out and works its way through lush vegetation until the last push up to the top, where one of the few remaining lookout towers stands guard. This view is gorgeous and makes one of the better places to eat lunch in the area.

Pyramid Peak isn't a tough climb. However, like nearly everything else on the Olympic Peninsula, the trail comes with elevation gain. With great views of the Strait of Juan de Fuca and Lake Sutherland, your view all around is unique and hard to beat. This is a great warm-up hike to some more-difficult trails later, or just a way to enjoy an afternoon with wonderful sights.

MILDRED LAKES

Mildred Lakes

Nearest City: Hoodsport
Best Season: All
How Far: 9 Miles
Elevation Gain: 2300ft

Directions:
From Hoodsport travel US 101 north for 14 miles. At milepost 318 turn left onto the Hamma Hamma River Road (Forest Road 25). Continue for 14 miles to the trailhead.

The trail to Mildred Lakes is nothing more than a fisherman's path that is more used by animals than by hikers, but the lack of traffic is what makes these lakes stand out from most of the others in the Olympic National Park. The trail is consistently overgrown, and despite volunteer groups cleaning it up, this trail is for the rugged few souls who want to brave the sometimes-difficult path. If you do venture down this trail, be prepared for isolated lakes that will take your breath away and make you wonder why the trail is forgotten about.

This trail should not be sugar-coated. It is a fantastic fishing hole tucked below the shadow of Mount Lincoln, but the route to the shores of this gorgeous mountain lake will make you think twice about the pay-off. However, even on a cloudy day, a day spent miles from everywhere, deep in the forests and mountains of the Olympic Peninsula make the rough slog completely worth it.

Upper Mildred Lake is one of the largest backcountry lakes on the Peninsula and needs to be seen. Between Mount Cruiser and Mount Pershing, these lakes are a perfect example of just how difficult travel was long ago on the Olympic Peninsula. Taking a hike up to the lakes will not only push you, but also give you an appreciation for the first people to explore in this beautiful land.

BUCKHORN LAKE

Buckhorn Lake

Nearest City: Sequim
Best Season: Summer/Fall
How Far: 12 Miles
Elevation Gain: 2000ft

Directions:
From Sequim, head East on Highway 101. Turn onto Louella Road. Turn left on Palo Alto Road. Bear right at a junction onto Forest Road 2880. The road descends and comes to another junction where you turn left on FR 2870. Bear right at a junction to continue on FR 2870 (formerly called FR 2860). Continue 10 miles to the trailhead.

Alpine lakes are spread out on the Olympic Peninsula, and just like the cities and people around Highway 101, each one is a little different. While some lakes are big or deep, Lake Buckhorn offers a perfect blend of swimmable waters and pretty views. Not too deep, the clear waters are fed by a picturesque waterfall through moss covered rocks. Lake Buckhorn isn't the prettiest of lakes, but it is more than worth the miles to get there.

The trail to get to Buckhorn Lake may become a personal favorite, as it skirts up from the Tubal Cain Mine area on switchbacks that offer great views of the interior of the Olympic Mountains. With deer, wildflowers, mountain goats and an occasional black bear sighting, the wide switchbacks offer a distraction from the elevation gain. The path gets a bit rough during the last half mile, but after dipping your feet in the lake, all the tired feelings go away.

Buckhorn Lake is also a great camping spot, so if you are looking for a place to start a backpacking trip, or just a remote overnight spot, this is it. During the winter, the snow in the area gets quite deep, so snowshoeing in isn't recommended. The summer months are perfect here, and if you catch it in the right spring conditions, wildflowers and rhododendrons will be blooming as far as the eye can see.

WAGONWHEEL
LAKE

Wagonwheel Lake

Nearest City: Hoodsport
Best Season: All
How Far: 6 Miles
Elevation Gain: 3200ft

Directions:
From Shelton travel north on US 101 to Hoodsport. Turn onto State Route 119 to a T intersection with Forest Road 24. Make a sharp left. In 1.7 miles the pavement ends. Continue on a good gravel road (FR 24) and in 3.7 miles come to a junction. Turn right and drive 1.2 miles to the Staircase Ranger Station.

Trails on the Olympic Peninsula do not get much steeper than the route up to Wagonwheel lake, but don't let the elevation climb stop you from experiencing this alpine lake. While not the greatest high-alpine lake in the Olympic Peninsula, this is a must-see due to the fact that so few take the time to hike it.

The trail is a perfect microcosm of the Olympic Peninsula. Starting at nearly sea level, the trail rises from the banks of one of the more lazy stretches of the Skokomish river, steadily climbing through dense forests, complete with old growth and giant ferns. While the trail rotates between switchbacks and slightly brutal climbs, it stands as a testament to human-kind's desire to see something new.

Wagonwheel Lake is a small lake between two rugged peaks, making it perfectly situated for a day of exploring, or just taking in a meal at a remote destination. Used by locals as a training hike for long trips, this trail isn't for beginning hikers. Wagonwheel Lake is a fantastic destination when you need something to do and is a great way to test just how in shape you are.

MOUNT ROSE

Mount Rose

Nearest City: Hoodsport
Best Season: All
How Far: 6.5 Miles
Elevation Gain: 3500ft

Directions:
From Shelton travel north on US 101 to Hoodsport. Turn onto State Route 119 to a T intersection with Forest Road 24. Make a sharp left. In 1.7 miles the pavement ends. Continue on FR 24 for 1 more mile to the trailhead, located on your right.

Located directly above Lake Cushman and within a stone's throw from the Olympic National Park's Staircase Entrance, Mount Rose sits atop a burned forest, exposing her craggy summit for the world to see. Mount Rose isn't the prettiest of mountains. In fact, she is often overlooked by tourists, hikers and climbers for more glamorous peaks located nearby. Being so close to Mount Ellinor and Mount Washington, Mount Rose is more of the middle child. Challenging, rewarding and serene, this peak nestled in the Southeast corner of the Olympic Mount Range, begging for your attention and love.

At a round-trip distance of 6.3 miles long and over 3,334 feet of elevation gained, Mount Rose is sure to get your legs a little sore. This is not for first-time hikers; and depending on the snow pack, you may need a GPS or route-finding skills to find the trail. The mountain should be snow-free from June to October, with August and September being the best time to climb.

If you are looking for sweeping vistas and a look into the interior of the Olympic Mountains, this is not the hike for you. That being said, Mount Rose does offer unique views of Mount Ellinor, Mount Washington, Copper Mountain, Cub Peak and on a clear day Mount Rainier, Mount Adams and Mount Saint Helens. At the end of the day, if you want a great elevation hike, Mount Rose is one of the best leg-burners on the Olympic Peninsula. Use this for a training hike; and after a few times up, you will be in decent shape.

ENCHANTED VALLEY

Enchanted Valley

Nearest City: Aberdeen
Best Season: Spring/
Summer
How Far: 26 Miles
Elevation Gain: 1300ft

Directions:
Head north on US 101
from Aberdeen. Turn
onto the South Shore
Road.
Proceed on this road for
13.5 miles, coming to a
junction at the Quinault
River Bridge.
Continue right,
proceeding 6.2 miles to
the road's end and the
trailhead.

If you have ever wanted to hike a marathon distance trail in the depths of one of the most beautiful rainforest in the world, this trail is for you. If you have ever wanted your destination to be waterfalls crashing down from giant hillsides or sitting on the porch of an old chalet, this hike is for you. Located in the middle of one of the more bear active areas in the Washington, the Enchanted Valley is a dream come true. This is a relatively flat trail to the land of bears, elk and waterfalls. Enchanted Valley is my personal favorite hike, and you will be hard pressed to find someone who has been here not describe it lovingly.

The trail itself can be muddy and occasionally quite buggy, but those are small distractions along a gorgeous path. The views along the way are great; the valley itself seems to be taken right out of a storybook. During the late spring, the cliffs and hills surrounding the valley erupt with waterfalls as far as the eye can see. (Some are pummeling down over 1,000 feet) It is common for first time hikers to sit in awe for hours. Resident black bears can and will be seen, so follow all posted signs and you will be safe.

Enchanted Valley will cast a spell on you. To most, it is hands-down the greatest destination in the Olympic National Park. There is some urgency to see this location, though, as The Chalet, built in the early 1930's, is a winter storm or two away from having the mighty Quinault River erode the final few feet of ground separating the river from the building. See it now, see it often. The Enchanted Valley along the Quinault River is a highlight for all, and should be a sought-after trek, no matter what the distance.

MORE INFORMATION ON THE OLYMPIC PENINSULA AND EXOTIC HIKES

Website: www.exotichikes.com

Twitter: @Exotichikes

Phone: 360.350.8938